Tiny Cat

by **Yoneo Morita**

CHRONICLE BOOKS
SAN FRANCISCO

Library of Congress Cataloging-in-Publication Data is available.

ISBN 978-1-4521-4975-2

Manufactured in China

Background photographs by Naomi Shirakawa
Planning by Mari Kiso (Eventas)
Design by Andrew Pothecary (forbidden colour)
Jacket and Case Design by Neil Egan
Editing and Production by Aki Ueda (Pont Cerise)
Rights Coordination by Rico Komanoya

10 9 8 7 6 5 4

Chronicle Books LLC
680 Second Street
San Francisco, CA 94107
www.chroniclebooks.com

Come play with me and my friends!

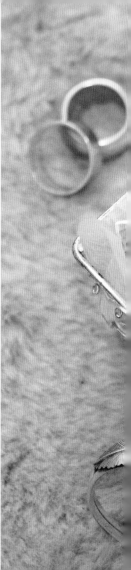

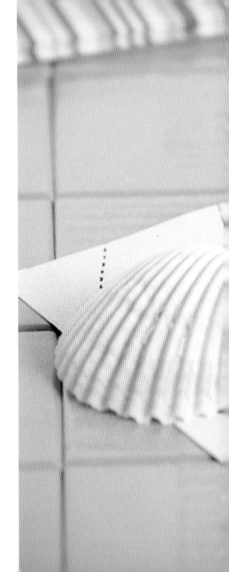

About the Photographer

Yoneo Morita has been photographing pets in playful ways for over 20 years. He has published more than 100 books and products, including his breakout *Hanadeka*—"big nose" in Japanese—series, which has been sold in over 40 countries around the world. This new Tiny series is his latest work featuring the irresistible *kawaii* nature of dogs and cats, which he loves most of all.

Yoneo currently lives in Tokorozawa, Japan, with his wife, one rabbit, three dogs, and eight cats.

Hello, I am

Tiny Cat

Place stamp here

From *Tiny Cat*, published by Chronicle Books LLC.